PINT SIZE ADVENTURER

-

The Abundant Adventure Creator™ PART 2

PAOLO BEN SALMI

aka

"Pint Size Adventurer"

AWARD WINNING AUTHOR &
The Youngest Ever Ambassador for
Water-to-Go™

AS SEEN ON TV, IN NEWSPAPERS & ON RADIO

ADVENTUROUS
PUBLISHING

Published by Adventurous Publishing in 2019

The author asserts the moral right under the Copyright, Designs and Patents Act to be identified as the author of this work.

ISBN: 978-1-913310-18-9

DEDICATION

I want to dedicate this book to children and their parents around the world who desire to go on adventures out in the wild and inwards adventures of self-discovery.

My mum and dad
Sabrina and Mohamed Ben Salmi.

My brothers and sisters:
Lashai Ben Salmi aka DREAMPRENEUR,
Tray-Sean Ben Salmi aka INFLUENCER,
Yasmine Ben Salmi, aka LOVEPRENEUR,
Amire Ben Salmi aka Mr INTELLIGENT.

Mary Paul my nan founder of Mary Paul's Creations.

Philip Chan 10 Seconds Maths Expert for editing the book and believing in me and helping us to share our books with the world.

FOREWORD

I met Paolo and his family at an event a few years ago and I knew then he was a child genius.

Their mother is what I would call a Personal Development junkie (In a very good way), she was always learning and growing but she was doing it with all of her five children. She took them to every event and every seminar there was going.

After our initial meeting, Paolo and the family very quickly became my soul family as well. Paolo was always very inquisitive, always asking questions, always exploring possibilities.

When he read a book I wrote, "Empower Yourself with 7 Natural Laws," he was very complimentary of the book and said it had inspired him to write his own book, "Pint Size Adventurer - 10 Key Principles To Get Your KIDS off Their iPads & Into The Wild."

Paolo's message here is very simple yet powerful not just for Kids but also for parents as well:

"You are a star and when someone tells you that your dream is too big or too small just say, I am who I am and who I choose to be. I believe in MYSELF no matter what"

Most of our children in society learn from their parents and to them we are their heroes growing up, they look to us for their every need. The challenge here is the things we lack and don't take care of they will inherit from us. Paolo Ben Salmi's book is a wakeup call for all families across the world to support them in getting back to the basic principle of life, which is living.

The world is our oyster and we can give, be, do and have whatever it is we want in life. It all starts with self-discovery and self-actualisation. It all starts with treating life as a game that we can play to win by becoming a "Pint Size Adventurer" it starts with us (parents) showing our children the way to have fun by getting out into nature (Wild) and connecting with her. It starts with (you) our child showing us the way to have fun again as a family unit.

iv

This book is a very practical book that brings families back together again. Paolo didn't achieve all of this by himself. He had the help, support and backing of his entire family.

Thank you, Paolo, for reminding us what is truly important in life (family). Parents get your priorities right!!! I highly recommend that every parent get this book for their children and read it together but not just reading it but also taking action and following through on some the great suggestions that Paolo has outlined to begin your adventures. These should definitely give YOU ideas for your own adventures.

You only have one life to live – And as far as I know, there are no trial runs in life. So, get out there into the wild and experience what it truly feels like to be alive. Learn to laugh more, play more, love more, give more, be more, do more and I promise you will have more, and your life will be more enriching and fulfilled.

It all starts here with this Pint Size Adventurer book series by Paolo Ben Salmi aka "Pint Size Adventurer"

The question is which adventure would you choose to take?

"There's two types of adventures, 1 going out into the wild and exploring and 2 going on an inwards journey of self-discovery" Paolo Ben Salmi aka Pint Size Adventurer

I would like to suggest that you make a decision today and for the rest of your life that you will become a "Pint Size Adventurer" and explore what possibilities life has in store for you. I will leave you with the words of a great mentor who loved the outdoor activities - Dare to dream and make each day an Epic Adventure!!!

Tosin Ogunnusi author of Empower Yourself with 7 Natural Laws and Time 2 Break Free. UK's Number 1 Empowerment Trainer and Executive Coach:
https://mpowerment.sendmedetails.com/nlp

CONTENTS

PAOLO BEN SALMI aka PINT SIZE ADVENTURER

8

ACKNOWLEDGMENTS

I would like to thank everyone who inspires me, encourages
me and helps me to become who I am today.

Thank you so much from my family and me.

A special thank you to:

**Daniel Barahona, Juan Pablo Barahona,
Regan Anne Hillyer** and your team
**Robyn Nikora, Stephen McGrath, The
Unstoppable Family (Rhonda Swan, Brian Swan
& Hanalei)
Marisa Lewis, Dave Shanks & Dominic Simms
from Water-to-Go™, Reginald Maynor via
Luster Products, Mucktaru Kargbo aka MK,
Malik Muhammad, Ben Green, Kallum Scott,
Andre Whyte, John Ndikum, Gary Hayes, Carl
Southwell CHELSEA F.C EDGE OF THE
BOX, Brunell University, Ash Dykes,
Tosin Ogunnusi, Jordan Wylie, Sunil Chuni,
Narelle Clyde, Lauren Till** and everyone else
who has helped us on our journey

**I want to convey my deep gratitude
to my publisher**

Adventurous Publishing

Our editor
PHILIP CHAN

Our family graphic designer
PRASANTHIKA MIHIRANI founder **SWISS GRAPHICS**

DISCLAIMER

Paolo Ben Salmi (the author) is a business and life coach/mentor. Nothing more and nothing less. The Author cannot, and do not, make any promises, guarantees, warrantees or representations about results other than the coaches diligent work with you. Advices are being provided "AS IS" without warranty of any kind, either express or implied, including without limitation any warranty for information, coaching, products or services provided through or in connection with this book. The advices in this book are requested at the coaching/mentoring participant's own choice and with inherent singular responsibility of the coaching/mentoring participant.

The author would like to explicitly point out that the advices that the author offer do not replace the expertise of a medical doctor or of an alternative non-medicine practitioner. Advices differ decidedly from those of a medical doctor or that of a practitioner in the non-medical area.

The author does not claim to make any diagnosis or give any promises of any sort of healing processes. The author is neither qualified nor equipped to deal with a person with pathological history, should you be in medical or psychiatric treatment due to any health issues, it is strongly advised to continue your therapy with your doctors. In case you still want to be coached/mentored by the author of this book, kindly consult your doctors before contacting the author. Whatever your decision, please do not interrupt your treatment with your doctor(s).

This book is focused on offering you a host of inspiration and resources to give you a chance to open your mind to the wonders of abundance in life for a more satisfying existence. This book will help you to learn how to loosen the control mechanisms that habitually stop us. For all other physical or mental health issues you are advised to consult professionals who are specifically trained to treat such challenges.

The author shall not be responsible for any loss or damage caused, or alleged to have been caused, directly or indirectly, by the information or ideas contained, suggested, or referenced in this book. However, if any legal relations arise in connection with this book, shall be governed by and construed in accordance with the laws of United Kingdom.

THE ABUNDANT ADVENTURE CREATOR™ Part 2

A MESSAGE FROM MY
HEART TO THE WHOLE WORLD

You are a star and when someone tells you that your dream is too big or too small just say

**"I am who I am
and who I choose to be.
I believe in MYSELF
no matter what!"**

THE ABUNDANT ADVENTURE CREATOR™

I am sure that you have been having lots of fun outside in the wild since reading my first book

Since writing my first book, I have been busy writing The Abundant Adventure Creator™ book, going on adventures, building relationships and creating my new system called the Abundant Adventure Creator™ and I am very excited to share this second edition of Pint Size Adventurer with you. My system is a workshop, mentoring, coaching and a 21 Day Challenge please get in touch for more information.

THE REAL LIFE REEL™

MYSTIC MAP MAKER™

RISE AND SHINE™

Here is a fun exercise that you can do with friends and family.

I really believe that the world is our stage and we can either be in the movie, we can watch the movie, or we can direct the movie. Whichever you choose is totally up to you, what matters most is that you take responsibility for your life by taking responsibility for your thoughts, feelings, words and actions, stop blaming, stop complaining, refuse to take anything personal, smile, make yourself happy, live in the present moment, use the power of intention, stay calm and confident

Take a moment to sit comfortably with your eyes closed, then take three deep breaths and notice how relaxed you become with each breath. Now take a deep breath in slowly and count 4 seconds, then hold your breath for 4 seconds, then slowly breath out and count of 4 seconds. Now I want you to create a picture of you living your dream lifestyle, hear what you hear, feel what you feel and see what you see and notice how that feels with every cell in your body.

1. write a list of things that you want to experience, buy or create.
2. make a list of your fears relating to your goals and negative thoughts that might make you think that you cannot achieve your goals.

 3. write a positive affirmation for each of your fears for example if you said, "I want to join a football team" and then you had a negative thought of "I am not good at football". You could write a positive affirmation like "I am getting better and better at football the more I practice". The most important part is to share your goals with your family and close friends so they can help you to achieve your goals.

HERE ARE SOME PHOTOS FROM MY LATEST ADVENTURES

What adventures have you been on? It would be super cool if you could share your adventure with me online via Facebook, Instagram and/or Twitter just search my name Paolo Ben Salmi

Stephen McGrath
Big Heart, Photographer & Videographer

www.maddoggiraffe.com

Passionate creative view on life expressed through my video,
photography and art.
Great when your job is more like a hobby.

I AM THE YOUNGEST EVER WATER-TO-GO™ AMBASSADOR

I feel so honoured to be the youngest ever Water-to-Go™ Ambassador. As a special gift you can get a huge 15% by using this discount code: BENSALMI when you visit my website:
www.watertogo.eu/paolobensalmi

Water-to-Go™ is a UK business set up by Dave Shanks back in 2010, with the aim to address two the largest problems facing the world: access to safe, clean drinking water and the pollution created by single-use plastics. After seeing the effects of plastic pollution first-hand, he sought to create a reusable and sustainable alternative to single-use plastic bottles. And so, Water-to-Go™ was born. Water-to-Go™ is a water filter bottle that eliminates well in excess of 99.9% of all microbiological contaminants including viruses, bacteria, chemicals, heavy metals as well as microplastics from any non-saltwater source in the world. The filters combine one traditional & two nano technologies delivering clean, safe drinking water from any non-saltwater source whether your journey takes you to the Gym, Glasgow or Ghana. Their mission is to create a commercially success business so that they can get the product to those who need it the most. To do this, they work with several organisations, ambassadors, partners and charities. One charity they are currently working that is making a huge difference is Malaria No More UK. Water-to-Go™

have produced a limited edition MNMUK branded bottle that they are selling via their website to raise money and awareness to help defeat malaria across the world. The bottles are being distributed and used all over the world by adventurers and explorers like Paolo, to provide safe, drinking water wherever they are and to help protect the planet from the damage caused by single-use plastic bottles. Together with Water-to-Go™, we can change the world, one bottle at a time. Ambassadors who share Paolo's love and enthusiasm for exploring and adventures.

LET ME TO INTRODUCE YOU TO SOME OF MY FELLOW AMBASSADORS AT WATER-TO-GO™

Chaz Powell
Water-to-Go™ Ambassador

www.thewildestjourney.com
www.instagram.com/thewildestjourney

One of them is Chaz Powell, a UK adventurer and expedition leader who has travelled to all different parts of the world and now lives his life through 'The Wildest Journey'. The Wildest Journey began with a curious intrigue that beckoned exploration. With the overwhelming draw of the unfamiliar, the journey was just too exciting to resist. It is his thirst in discovering or learning something new that drives him and embarking on his wildest journeys marked the beginning of a new series of exciting exploration-based adventures and challenges.

"I'm pretty sure I always wanted to explore. But mainly my local woodlands and hills in Shropshire. I was always begging my father to take me to the wild places near our home. Just so I could spend time walking in nature. It's definitely something that's always been rooted inside me. To take adventures. Big and small. Then as time went by that urge grew and I started to want to visit mountains and camp out in the wild areas further afield. It's always been an ever-growing progression throughout my life."

"I have been on adventures here in the UK and abroad but have recently mainly focussed on African adventures, in particular walking Africa's rivers. The best adventure I have been on was walking the length of the Zambezi River. From August 2016 until September 2017 I took on a huge personal walk, hiking the Zambezi from its Source to the Indian Ocean; completing 3000 km by foot over a duration of 137 days, solo and unsupported and completing my dream journey."

"My next adventure is trekking the length of the Gambia River which will be an exciting but challenging journey starting in Guinea, taking me through Senegal and across Gambia to Banjul along the country's west coast. Following this, I hope to also be able to walk the Rift Valley in the future as well."

"Water-to-Go™ is a product that has breathed new life into my expeditions over the past few years and is now one of the most crucial pieces of kit that I carry whilst out on my many remote and wild journeys. It has changed the way I look at adventure, allowing me to venture further into more and more inaccessible regions, but yet still obtain safe clean drinking water without the worry of becoming sick or seriously dehydrated.

Jordan Wylie
Water-to-Go™ Ambassador

www.jordanwylie.org

Jordan Wylie is a former soldier, bestselling author, extreme adventurer and also one of the stars of Channel 4's BAFTA nominated shows *Hunted* and *Celebrity Hunted.*

Growing up on the largest council estate in the UK, Jordan left school early with no qualifications to his name but took the life-changing decision to join the British Army at 16 years old. He served for ten years and saw Operational Service in Northern Ireland and Iraq where he specialised in military intelligence, reconnaissance and surveillance operations. On leaving the Army, Jordan entered the world of Maritime Security, making headlines after armed

Somali pirates boarded a ship that he was protecting and Jordan found himself in charge and forced to make critical decisions for the safety of his crew. It was this experience that led Jordan to write "Citadel: The True Story of One Man's War Against the Pirates of Somalia", which became a bestseller on publication in 2017.

Jordan has since gone on to successfully complete numerous major charity expeditions, including the highly publicised Running Dangerously, which saw him run through Afghanistan, Iraq and Somalia, and Barefoot Warrior which involved climbing Mt Kilimanjaro, Africa's highest mountain, completely barefoot! He has raised over a million pounds for charity and some of his expeditions have been made into documentaries on Sky TV. Since his time in the military, Jordan has battled with severe depression, chronic anxiety and epilepsy, and now campaigns to remove the stigma from people suffering from mental illness.

In recent years, Jordan has also returned to education, proving it doesn't matter where you start in life, there is always the opportunity to assert yourself and try again, he now holds a BA (Hons) and MA in the field of Security and Risk Management where he is an industry thought leader and commentator in the mainstream media with regular appearances on Sky News and the BBC.

Ash Dykes Reaches
Halfway Point in #MissionYangtze
Water-to-Go™ Ambassador

www.ashdykes.com
www.faceboo.com/AshDykesOfficial

Guinness Book of Record Holder and UK adventurer and Water-to-Go™ ambassador, Ash Dykes, has reached the halfway point of his massive mission to trek the entire length of China's Yangtze River. Despite everything that has been thrown at him, Ash has continued to make excellent progress and has already completed half of his third world-first and biggest mission to date.

Ash has walked 2000 miles along the river to reach this huge milestone, and along the way has faced all kinds of life-threatening dangers (landslides, bears and being tracked by a pack of wolves) as well as being held up 5 times by police/government officials. Death-defying extreme athlete Ash Dykes reached safety at the halfway point of his mammoth world first expedition 9th January 2019, having faced immense threats to his safety whilst attempting to walk the entire length of China's Yangtze River in just a year.

Having set off on 26th August 2018, Ash has battled the elements and overcome many obstacles to get to where he is now. There have been several times where Ash has feared for his life but has relied on his intense training regimes and wild instincts to get him through a tough first half of the expedition. Despite many tough moments, he has always had the confidence and reassurance to trust his to deliver clean, safe drinking water to keep him hydrated through his mission.

Olie Hunter Smart
Water-to-Go™ Ambassador

www.oliehuntersmart.com
www.facebook.com/oliehuntersmart

Olie Hunter Smart is UK adventurer who left his desk job in 2013 and rekindled his passion for adventure and travel; backpacking all over the world. He now also speaks to different organisations, schools, and at shows about his adventures to educate and inspire the next generation of explorers.

"When I was younger the curtains in my bedroom were of a jungle scene - cartoon lions, giraffe, gorillas and so on, surrounded by lush green plants. I can imagine them right now. These were my parents' choice and I honestly can't remember anything different. As a 9-year-old I wanted to visit the jungle and see some of these animals for real (little did I know that lions and giraffe don't live in the jungle!). Over time, I grew an interest in the outdoors through things like the scouts and DofE, having to arrange our own mulit-day expeditions. My interest in geography and the environment also grew as I studied, right through to degree level."

"At the age of 18, after I'd completed my A-levels, I couldn't imagine anything else than taking a year out to go travelling. I wanted to see the world and experience different cultures, see new landscapes that I'd only seen in pictures and on TV. And where should I go? To experience the scene, I grew up with on my childhood curtains, the jungle of course! I found an organisation that took people of a similar age out to Belize, work on a conservation project and live in a village, teaching in a local school. That was my first experience of a very different place to the one I'd grown up in, understanding how people live in different and challenging environments."

"The jungle is my favourite environment to be in and I've been lucky enough to visit jungles in Belize, Malaysia, Indonesia, Singapore, Australia, NZ, India, Peru and Brazil. Perhaps it all stems from those curtains that I grew up with as a kid!"

"The best adventure I went on was in April 2017 when I set off on a solo journey over 4,500km to walk the length of India to uncover untold stories of Independence and Partition. It was an amazing trip to follow in Gandhi's footsteps. I have other adventures on the way, possibly not as long as this one!"

"I've used Water-to-Go™ for several years, particularly when I undertake a big expedition, and I must say, I can't fault them! I've drunk water straight out of the Amazon River for 3 months using their bottles, as well as spending 9 months in India topping up wherever I could find. Even the locals advised me against drinking water in some places, but I was confident that the Water-to-Go™ bottle would protect me. And I'm pleased to say that I've returned without any water-based issues! Plus, it helps save the planet as there are no single-use bottles flying about, and you save money too."

"My message to all young adventurers is don't let things get in the way of what you want to do or achieve. Travel is the best way to learn more about the world and about yourself so I would recommend it to everyone."

Global Convoy
Water-to-Go™ Ambassador

www.globalconvoy.com
www.instagram.com/globalconvoy

Global Convoy are a group of adventurers and travel enthusiasts who explore the world on overloading adventures. The main team consists of Max, Becca and Joel wanted to create a way in which people could sign up and go on an adventure that would suit their needs, time and budget. The unlikely catalyst that would eventually bring the Convoy team together was the Mongol Rally, otherwise described as the 'The Greatest Motoring Adventure On The Planet'. Following that, the original Global Convoy was a 'Round The World' overlanding adventure which crossed 4 continents, 46 countries, 5 deserts, 5 seas and 7 mountain ranges and it had hundreds of different people - from 33 different nationalities - involved from beginning to end. Ever since then, they have been going on other overloading adventures that anyone can join and get involved with.

Becca - "When I was 9, I loved history and had a high interest in the natural wonders of the world. I dreamed about travelling to them and seeing them in their element, with all the magical flora. My interest in culture and nature has lead me to where I am now and drives my passion for adventure. I feel at home when outdoors and having the ability to continue learning about the world is a dream come true."

Max - "When I was 9 all my adventures were in the realm of make believe. I wanted to ride dinosaurs, live on a mountain top and be a pirate. What I didn't know was that a lot of my childhood adventures are more realistic than I thought! There may not be as many dinosaurs as I planned but all I've learnt growing up is that there's so much more adventure all around than I could have ever imagined!"

Joel - "At age 9 I read many books based on the adventures of Shackleton in the Antarctic. The idea of exploring parts of the world completely unknown to any others was always something that captured my imagination. While it's hard to find places completely unknown on this planet, you can still discover new things that YOU never knew going to the places most people don't! The basis of this is what continues to fuel my ambition to travel today."

"Our favourite adventure was our round the world trip crossing 4 continents with a huge group of us. It was an amazing experience and we would definitely recommend it. We have several other convoy trips planned mainly around Europe but some others further afield."

"We have been lucky enough to have our Water-to-Go™ bottles for our journeys in Europe and across the world; we found ourselves cutting our costs by filling up from waterfalls, lakes and rivers. Water-to-Go™ was literally a life saver. It allowed us to carry all our gear and not have to worry about lugging around litres of water. This convenience allowed us to focus our time on absorbing the culture rather than worrying about when we would next find drinking water."

This is a letter about me from Dave Shanks who's the founding director of Water-to-Go™.

To Whom it may concern.

Water-to-Go has a policy of appointing a small number of 'ambassadors' for our water filter bottles. These ambassadors are chosen to represent our products because of their experience, attitude and consideration for the planet. The decision is not taken lightly and in most cases falls to myself as CEO.

On Saturday 10th November 2018, Water-to-Go attended The Commonwealth Fair 2018 organised by the Commonwealth Countries League, in aid of the Commonwealth Girls Education Fund. The event was held at Kensington Town Hall in London. During the event, I was approached by Paolo Ben Salmi, aka Pint Size Adventurer. Paolo explained about his love for everything outdoors, and his quest to encourage young people to get out and about to explore the natural world. Not only does this resonate with Water-to-Go, but Paolo's enthusiasm for protecting the environment, made him an ideal candidate to join our elite group of ambassadors.

After discussing the opportunity with his inspirational mother, Sabrina, Water-to-Go has appointed Paolo to be their youngest ever ambassador at just 9 years old.

As an example of Paolo's enthusiasm, the day after his Water-to-Go website went live: https://www.watertogo.eu/paolobensalmi Paolo managed to secure an interview on London Live 1st December 2018 featuring our branded bottle. I would encourage any institution, event or corporation to meet this young man. He is and will further develop to become an inspiration for youngsters across the world. We are both delighted and proud to work with him.

Dave Shanks

Best regards,

Dave

Dave Shanks
Founder / Director
+44 1582 841412
+44 7711 425546

www.watertogo.org

Water-to-Go Ltd
Unit 8, The Workshops,
Greenfield Road,
Pulloxhill, Bedfordshire
MK45 5BF
United Kingdom

Water-to-Go™ wrote this amazing blog about me, if you would like to read the full blog please visit: www.watertogo.eu/blog/meet-paolo-Water-to-Go™s-youngest-ever-ambassador/

January 18, 2019 | By Water-to-Go.

Meet Paolo: Water-to-Go's youngest ever ambassador

Multiple award-winning Paolo Ben Salmi, aka Pint Size Adventurer, is not your average 9 year old – he is a public figure, speaker, former radio host, author and now Water-to-Go's youngest ever ambassador!

Water-to-Go is delighted to be working with Paolo to prove that age is just a number when you want to make a difference. The idea and tagline behind Pint Size Adventurer was to show that 'Together We Can Explore The World.' He believes that there should be no boundaries in the way of travelling and exploring the world so he is the perfect person to promote and inspire

I really love being a Water-to-Go™ Ambassador because their mission is to protect:

- Protect their customers' health and well-being by offering safe, healthy water anywhere in the world

- Protect our planet by offering an environmentally friendly reusable alternative to single-use plastic water bottles

- Protect their customers' finances by delivering clean water at a fraction of the cost of bottled water

Use Water-to-Go™ products and you'll be healthier, wealthier and helping to make the World a better place!

Dave Shanks, CEO and Founder of Water-to-Go™, explains why he started the business in 2010 and how Water-to-Go™ provides a solution to two of the biggest problems in the world: access to clean, safe drinking water and the pollution caused by single-use plastics.

WHY ME & MY FAMILY USE A WATER-TO-GO™ BOTTLE?

Before I joined the Water-to-Go™ team I always forgot to drink water when I was at school, now I drink more water because it is clean and fresh, so it feels and tastes good, so I now drink more water.

Did you know that Water-to-Go™ Keeps You Healthy

Our unique water filtration system protects you by removing things that are bad for you while keeping good stuff like minerals in the water that you drink. A Water-to-Go™ filter will:

• Remove chemicals in your tap water such as chlorine and fluoride
• Take out contamination from untreated water sources either at home or abroad
• Stop viruses, bacteria and water borne cysts entering your digestive system
• Keep you free from BPA

What Does BPA-Free Mean?

BPA (Bisphenol A) is a chemical compound found in many single-use water bottles. Medical reports show some of these plastic water bottles 'leach' man-made oestrogen (BPA) into its contents when the bottle is exposed to sunlight or temperatures over 60°F or 15°C. These oestrogens can lead to cancer. That means leaving a bottle in your car or outside a shop, in sunlight, starts the process!
The materials we use are LDPE and PET, specially selected materials which are FDA-approved for food and beverages. It cannot leak or taint the water and has been specifically designed to be BPA-free. **This makes our products reusable, refillable and 100% recyclable.**

The Health Benefits of Hydration

Water makes up around 70% of us. It helps the body function, maintaining physical and mental health. Drinking water and staying hydrated is a vital component of any good health and fitness plan. Latest research recommends that an average adult should consume 4-6 litres of water daily. More than 80% of us fail to come close to the target: we tend to ignore water until the time we feel thirsty.
Here's why hydration (drinking water) is good for your health:

Hydration keeps you active

Water is necessary for the body. It is the one thing that can keep you going for an extended period without feeling tired. According to experts, drinking water at regular intervals can help improve alertness and helps keep the body active. Taking in water periodically forces the body to recalibrate the electrolytic balance of fluids in the body for optimum use.

Hydration helps in detoxification

Our body is a machine that works by continuously breaking down complex chemical compounds into simpler forms and converting them to energy. The entire process of assimilation of nutrients consumed by the body produces a number of toxins and waste products. These accumulate in the body and are then excreted out in a number of ways. As you sip a glass of water, you are giving your system the additional buffer to reduce the effect of toxins, process them and then flush these waste products away.

Hydration slows aging

The self-regulatory mechanism of our bodies performs much more efficiently when all the components it needs are there for it to use. Drinking plenty of water is good for the skin, and healthy skin is a sign of looking younger.

Since water helps in removing toxins from the system, problems like acne and excessive oil accumulation in the skin pores, are much more easily dealt with by a better hydrated body.

Hydration helps in regulating body temperature

Thermoregulation is the process of keeping the body within an optimal temperature range, so that it is neither too hot nor too cold. The most obvious example is sweating, where water is pumped through the skin and then the body's heat energy helps evaporate the sweat. This has a cooling effect that lowers body temperature.

Water is an essential component for the body's methods of thermoregulation.

Hydration helps improve digestion

Feeding the body, the nutrients it requires to function (digestion) uses water at every stage. A lack of water results in less efficient assimilation of food and less effective of the body's energy stores. Drink more water and you will better process fat. With more energy you will feel better too.

Hydration improves brain function

The human brain works by generating and replicating electrical impulses. This entire system functions using the electrolyte ions present in the body. Electrolyte ions are made available in fluids that are primarily water. The brain is more water than almost any other organ (roughly 80% water in composition) so having access to water from the body helps it to work in the best possible manner. So there are at least 6 reasons why being fully hydrated makes you healthier. Having a Water-to-Go™ filter bottle at hand supports you in staying hydrated, taking out a huge range of things that are bad for you whilst allowing you to drink healthy water wherever you are.

FIND YOUR ADVENTURE

Adventurers are not only about going outside and finding treasure.

At times it's about finding the answer to a question. An adventure could also be about going on an adventure of self-discovery to find the treasure that is buried deep within YOU.

I love these types of adventures because discovering oneself is the best discovery ever.

Often adults can live their entire lives without knowing who they really are.
This are so many lonely and heartbroken people in the world.

The good thing is that things do not have to be like this is because YOU can choose to go on an adventure into the wild outdoors and/or an inward adventure of self-discovery right now.

GET OFF YOUR IPADS AND GET INTO THE WILD!...

YOU HAVE TWO OPTIONS

1) An adventure outdoors

2) An adventure inwards of self-discovery

The question is which adventure will you choose to go on today?

Let's face it there is no getting away from the advantages of having access to technology. Technology is now essential for everyday life and children's education.

Mobile phones allow us to maintain communication when we are away from home.

Life has become an experience of access at a click of a button for us children.

We can do homework online, connect with family & friends on skype, find entertainment at the press of a button and research information on just about anything.

But would you agree that too much screen time can have many disadvantages?

Some children spend 24 hours a day in front of a screen by the age of 7. So, what can we do to reduce the amount of time spent in front of the TV, surfing the internet, chatting on Facebook or playing games on a computer and/or mobile etc?

Shhh…
I AM GOING TO SHARE SOME INSIDE SECRETS WITH **YOU** ON HOW TO TEACH YOUR PARENTS THE 10 Key Principles To Get KIDS off Their iPads & **Into The WILD**

Reading this book will help you and your parents to make changes to your screen time.

Many families swing between being determined to reduce screen time and giving in for the sake of so-called peace and quiet.

It would benefit you most to make good decisions about the **habits and qualities** YOU want long-term and reduce your use of technology and spend more time in the WILD.

This will be good for YOUR development for the months and years ahead. Just like everything else in life finding **a healthy balance is key.**

After all there are going to be days that prove to be difficult and other days when things are in flow. So, I believe that by agreeing on some rules will help on those not so good days.

Focus on your **desired outcome** because you genuinely want the best for your whole family and reducing your screen time is a habit well-worth working together for.

Let's face it to begin with YOU will not be happy when screen time is reduced but one day just like me, YOU will not miss it and eventually be thankful for the change.

I used to be very upset, angry and at times I would have a tantrum when I first had to reduce screen time, but over time I learned to appreciate the time I had available to read, play outdoors and so much more in replacement of screen time.

The secret is consistency with the new rules, and you could have one of the biggest impacts on yours and your families connection, long-term intelligence, fitness and mental health and so much more.

Let's get started with my 10 Key Principles (*Please feel free to join me on Facebook: Pint Adventurer – Together We Can Explore The World to share your opinions*).

9yr old Paolo Ben Salmi aka Pint Size Adventurer

PRINCIPLE #1 IT IS GOOD TO TALK

I can remember a saying and it goes something like this

"It is always good to talk".

BECAUSE WE CANNOT READ PEOPLE'S MIND.

It's not good to assume because you could be wrong, so it's always better to ask

Principle 1 is very important because our parents understand more than we do and can explain things to us in a way we can easily understand. I think it is a very good idea to talk to your parents about the negative impact of too much screen time.

I have done a lot of research on this topic and I have learned that if you focus too much on watching people doing what you want to do you will never achieve what you want in life.

After all you always have three choices:

1) You can either watch the movie

2) You can either be in the movie

3) Last, but not least you can either direct the movie

For example, you dream of becoming a mathematician.
You then to watch other mathematicians in action, yes that would help you to learn.
Telling other mathematicians how to do what they do would help you to learn.

But, if you choose to practice, ask questions, get help from a tutor then you have an excellent chance of learning much more.

What would happen if you just choose to watch football, tell others how to swim spend most of your time playing video games?

Can you see how you can really waste your time only watching the things that do not help you to become a mathematician?

The question is which one do you often choose?

I am 9 years old so I know and understand how much fun you can have on computers, games consoles, mobile phones, iPads, TVs and iPods etc so I know that it is not easy to reduce your screen time without knowing how to do so. So, in this book I will teach you how to reduce your screen time successfully.

I know that technology is now essential for our education because we use them to communicate with our friends and family online, our favourite films, cartoons, learn a new language, research homework and play.

Can you imagine life without computers, games consoles, mobile phones, iPads, TVs and iPods etc?

You only need to ask your parents because they were born during the dinosaur ages (that's a joke Ha! Ha! Ha!...), they did not have what we have today.

Shhhh.... Don't tell them what I said It will be our little private joke. I used to ask to use a mobile phone, iPad, iPod, watch TV and to go online every day. I am proud to say that I have managed to reduce my screen time.

Now I do not ask to use them as much as I use to.

Now I spend a reduced amount of screen time and I still have lots of fun because there is so many things to do in life.

When our parents were our age, they did not have access to these things. I don't know about you but, I often hear adults talking about how much fun they had during their childhood doing things such as playing board games, marbles, skipping, hide and seek, riding a bike and using their imagination, learning with their families and friends both indoors and outdoors.

Nowadays so much is accessible at a click of a button for example online gaming, movies, online shopping etc.

Did you know that some children spend all day in front of some sort of a screen, do some research to see what you discover?

Talk to your parents about fun and exciting ways to reduce the amount of time you spend in front of a screen?

I also think that it would be a clever idea to talk to your parents about the negative effects that too much screen time will have on their **FINANCES** and your **INTELLIGENCE, PHYSICAL HEALTH, SOCIALISING** and **MENTAL HEALTH**.

Too much screen time can have a negative effect on
your **PARENTS FINANCES:**

- Have less money due to constant persuasion
  by advertisers to be materialistic and purchase
  the latest technology advertised
- It could increase your parents' electricity bill
  because it has to be charged and powered
  during usage
- You might constantly ask your parents to
  purchase the latest technological gadgets
  release.
- More likely to spend money on mobile
  phones, iPods, apps, computer games, games
  consoles etc. which are much more expensive
  than traditional toys, board games and arts
  and crafts etc.
- Discuss with your family and friends how you
  can reduce the amount money your parents
  spend on technology?

Too much screen time can have a negative effect on your **INTELLIGENCE** because you are:

- More likely to spend less time concentrating on your homework and school projects, and have difficulty focussing on work that requires your full attention for extended periods
- More likely to watch TV throughout the day
- More likely to achieve lower grades
- Less able to focus on skill-based activities such as creative arts, playing an instrument or sports
- More likely to have an unhealthy reading habit
- More likely to have a reduced attention span and experience frequent boredom due to expectation of instant entertainment and quick moving images such as those found on TV and electronic games
- More likely to spend less time using your imagination, little time being self-lead, little interest in participating in outdoor activities which are all vital for your cognitive development.

For example

If you want to learn how to play the piano, you will need to learn to spend less time playing video games and more time practicing how to read music and practice playing the piano keys.

I believe that the key to success is practice, because practice makes improvement and play is practice.

Ask yourself what have you been spending your life practising?

Whatever you spend your time doing, you will become better at.

Always remember that whatever you fight for you get to keep.

Discuss with your family and friends how you can improve your focus and create balance between screen time, play and homework?

Too much screen time can have a negative effect on your **PHYSICAL HEALTH:**

- You are more likely to become overweight due to the lack of daily exercise
- You are likely to become tired because you are spending too much time spent in front of screens
- You may have trouble falling asleep at bedtime because of electrical and light stimulation in your brain
- You may develop a tendency to snack on junk food whilst in front of a screen
- Too much screen time can lead to you being influenced by adverts for junk foods and drinks
- You increase your risk of heart disease, high blood pressure, diabetes and unhealthy sleep patterns (insomnia) due to extended periods of screen time
- You will become less energetic when you have too much screen time

- Too much screen time will decrease your muscles and make you unfit and unhealthy
- You will increase your chances of long-term back pain due to poor posture and need to contact our aunty Giselle to book your Alexander session
- You become more likely to develop repetitive strain injuries.
- Too much screen time has a negative effect on your eyesight due to extended periods focussing on a screen and not using the eye muscles to focus on long-distance objects, and flashing imagery often associated with TV and computer games

Did you know that there is a saying that wealthy people have huge book libraries and unhealthy people have huge TV screens?

Discuss with your family and friends how you can create balance to improve your physical health?

Too much screen time can have a negative effect on your **MENTAL/EMOTIONAL HEALTH:**

- Too much screen time can make you become anxious
- Too much screen time can lead to an addition to TV, computer games and social network sites etc
- Too much screen time can lead to you becoming disconnected from your emotions because if you are exposed to bad language, violence and/or abusive content your brain will normalise this and you will grow to be emotionless which could lead to profound consequences such as hurting yourself and/or other emotionally/physically.
- You become what you expose yourself to
- Always remember that you ae a powerful creator and thoughts becomes things. So, take responsibility for how you spend your spare time

- You can become attracted to a negative crowd of people due to the images that you view in video games
- You can increase your chances of depressed mental health and bad mood swings due to reduced exposure to sunlight and movement. Due to decreased physical face-to-face social interactions. Some children form addictions and watch the social activities and posts happiness of other children and grow resentful.
- You are at risk of having poor relationship and coping mechanisms
- You are more likely to become disconnected from reality. Children who spend a lot of time in front of a screen can have trouble separating fact from fiction and mistaking game mastery for success and control
- Children who spend too much time online increase their chances of experiencing cyber bullying especially if they participate in online chat rooms, instant messaging, online games and texts etc
- More likely to be involved in or view 'happy slapping' (filming the bullying of another child)
- More likely to view inappropriate content and be exposed to disturbing images and adult material which can destroy your childhood innocence

- More likely to develop serious problems due to poor social skills.

Did you know that the mind cannot tell the difference between what is reality and what you visualise?

Discuss with your family and friends how you can create balance to improve your mental/emotional health?

Too much screen time can have a negative effect on your **SOCIAL LIFE**

- You are more likely to have fewer close friendships of people who do not spend extended periods in front of the screen due to less time spent strengthening those friendships
- This could have a negative impact on your social skills such as your speech, listening, debating, negotiating and conflict resolution skills due to less time socialising with friends and family and too much screen time will interfere with conversations and discussion making
- Too much screen time can affect the quality time that you ought to be spending with family and friends. Which will reduce your understanding of traditional family values, morals and manners which contribute towards your social development and interactions

- Often children develop unhealthy habits of making critical remarks, anti-social jokes, and view harassment and intolerance as amusing due to viewing programmes, reality shows and comedies which present this as acceptable behaviours
- **Too much screen time can lead to you becoming aggressive because of the extended exposure to aggression and violent images**
- You may become more irritable, this is because of extended periods of inactivity, this leads to a build-up of adrenaline and suppressed emotions each time you become angry due to a build-up in energy with no physical release. Arguments, tantrums and sibling
- fights are more frequent after extended periods of time in front of a screen.

Discuss with your family and friends how you can create balance to improve your social life?

PRINCIPLE #2 MOVE TECHNOLOGY OUT OF THE BEDROOM

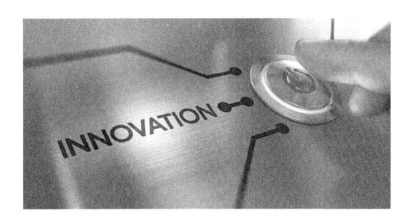

I believe that it is a very good idea to either remove all technology from the bedroom.

If for any reason this is not possible, you should agree on a reasonable length of time for screen time in the bedroom and at least two hours before bedtime.

Once a technology usage rule has been agreed upon for your bedroom it would be a good idea to come up with consequences if the rule is broken.

Before my family and I made the decision to reduce our screen time, we were just a typical family of seven online, using mobile phones, iPads, desktops, laptops, TVs, online and games consoles etc.

However, now that we know the benefits of living a lifestyle with reduced screen time.

We have benefited in so many ways because the time that we use to spend sitting in front of some sort of screen.

We now use to spend quality time together talking, playing chess, writing books, creating products and services, speaking on stage, hosting workshops, walking, creating, planning, discussing the things we are grateful for and hearing about each of our daily experiences.

So, you see that by simply removing technology out of your bedroom for bedtime could have an amazing impact on your health because you will eventually develop a healthier sleeping pattern because you will no longer be tempted to watch TV or use technology until way past your bedtime.

Me and my brother, use to enjoy watching a bedtime movie, playing on our iPads, mobiles etc. The bad thing is that I would fall asleep way past my bedtime and watching that movie or playing some sort of game would just make my brother want to stay up even later to watch and/or play another game.

Would you agree that technology has a way of captivating our attention? Have you ever tried to call someone who was focused on the TV screen and it was like they were hypnotised because you had to call them several time or you may have been the one they were trying to call but you could not even hear them?

Let's face it, no one sets out to spend 5-10 hours day online, using the mobile, watching television and on the iPad etc.

Let's be honest the temptation of technology is a hard one to fight off. So, to make matters easier simply remove technology from the bedroom.

Did you know that there are studies that say that watching TV just before bedtime actually disrupts your sleep cycles, do some research.

I did some research and I learned that getting good sleep at night is very important for your health.

Did you know that what you think about just before you fall asleep matters? Because it will either help you to have a good or bad dream.

Just before bedtime is an excellent opportunity to reflect on your day, relax, think happy thoughts and meditate.

When we choose to reflect on our day we can learn from our mistakes and acknowledge our achievements too.

When you wake up in the morning what is the first thing you think about?

Every morning you can choose to see it as the present it is instead of waking up and watching TV as soon as you open your eyes and allowing technology to control your actions and thoughts with their own agenda.

Be wise and take control of your life by becoming the captain of your ship by carefully choosing what you desire to experience in your day ahead instead of allowing technology to choose for you.

Would you agree that everything in our lives has a purpose? For example, legs are for walking, mouths are for talking, kitchens are for cooking, toy are for playing etc.

Would you agree that it might be a good idea to choose to use your bedroom for its purpose of sleeping by removing technology from your bedroom so you can get a good night's rest and wake up well rested the following morning.

- Did you know that if you do not choose to work towards your dreams someone else will make you work towards theirs?

- Did you know that during the evening is an excellent opportunity for you to use to catch up with your family unless, you choose to spend this quality time with technology?

Less watching and more talking is what I think would be a good choice to make just before bedtime. Instead of staring at a screen why not stare into the eyes of a family member.

- Did you know that children who have access to technology in their bedrooms score lower on school tests and are more likely to have sleep problems. Having access to technology in the bedroom is associated with sleeping problems etc.

There are some many benefits of not having a TV/technology in your room. For example, your television takes up space. Removing technology from your bedroom will create more space in your room.

- Did you know too much TV creates unrealistic expectations as TV rarely depicts the world and life accurately. Which results in disillusionment about what to expect from the world around us. This can be most detrimental to our relationships when the unrealistic expectations are applied to us personally, to our family, to our friends, to our education etc.

- Did you know that technology devices tend to be dust magnets? All electronics attract and trap dust.

Dust is not good for your health so why attract more dust?

I really believe that technology was designed to distract us from being creative because I remember not wanting to do anything else other than watch TV, play on my iPad, mobiles and other technology etc and I would always have a tantrum when asked to turn it off.

I remember reading somewhere that our brains are the smartest computer in the world, which made me feel that the addition to technology is an attack of our brain because it makes us focus outside of ourselves instead of inwards and focusing how to better use our brains as we mature.

Don't get me wrong technology has its benefits but addition to anything will have long last consequences.

Sadly, people who are addicted to technology will not know they are addicted until they have a break from technology and notice the unhealthy pull towards technology.

- Did you know that you can increase your speed of getting ready in the morning without a TV to distract you in the morning?

Why not swap your screen time for reading time at least it will make you smarter. I have put together some content for a 21 Day Challenge to help you achieve this, please see details of this at the back of my book. Just imagine how many more books you will be able to finish if you were to read more.

- Did you know that too much expose to static energy from your technology devices can have an adverse effect on your body.

My mum threw away our microwave after being affected by radiation poisoning and lots

of technology devices means high electricity bills?

Oh yeah have you heard the saying something along the lines of where your attention goes, energy begins to flow, and results will soon start to show?

Your attention is valuable and should be spent focusing on the special people in your life and on creating your dreams that deserve your undivided attention every single day.

Reducing your screen time will grant you extra time to do just that.

At least give it a try because you have nothing to lose and so much to gain.

Just imagine how much better your life could be when you make a decision to reduce your screen time.

PRINCIPLE #3
TIME IS PRECIOUS

- Why is time so precious?

I really believe that time is precious because you can't create more time, you can't earn more time, you don't get more time by being rich or poor, happy or sad, good or bad.

This is why I think time is precious.
One day everyone will run out of time, but no one knows when their time will run out.
Time running out is a part of our life cycle and life constantly reminders us to spend our time wisely.

- Did you know that when we learn how precious something is, we then learn to appreciate it more?

- Do you feel that it is wise to spend your time watching others live their dreams, watching

TV and playing games. Is that the best way to spend your time?

- What could you do differently with your precious time each day?

- What could you spend time creating?

- What would you spend time exploring and learning?

Each time you choose to spend your precious time saying or doing something disempowering your life is ticking by, and you will never get the time back.

At least if you are doing something that is empowering you can feel that you've spent your time wisely.

Here's the thing using your time wisely means different things to different people.
We are all very different and so we find different things to be of benefit to us.

For example, you may choose to spend your precious time with friends and family, or you may choose to out in nature exploring or be indoors creating.

Whatever it is for you I think that as long as you are following your heart that is what matters

most. All I am saying is that it would be a good idea to spend less time in front of a screen and more time BEING and experiencing this amazing life that you have been gifted.

So, you do not regret it later in life, they say that we tend to regret what we do not do instead of what we have done.

- Did you know that life can be so much easier when we choose to be present. Instead of hanging on to the past, instead you could choose to learn from the past and move forward into your future.

The results in your life will be determined by the things you choose to spend your precious time focusing on.

For example, if you spend time watching TV, watching others play, reading social media feeds, watching what others do in their lives, waiting to read what others think and say about you.

The question is what results will you now choose to work towards? And how will you choose to spend your time now that you have a better understanding of just how precious time is. What can you spend your time talking about, practicing, learning, creating, building, teaching, growing, cooking, tasting, writing, discovering, exploring, experiencing, questioning, investigating, researching, discovering, doing and with who?

I believe that you should learn to prioritise your time wisely, so you spend less time on social media and gaming and instead you spend more quality time with your family. I also think that you should encourage your parents to limit their own use of screen time, so they can lead you by example.

I also believe that you should spend your time wisely because once you waste it you can never get it back.

ACTIVITY TIME: At the end of the day draw a line down the middle of an A4 sheet of paper. On one side write 'What did I spend my time saying and doing today? and on the other side write 'What do I now choose to spend my time saying and doing tomorrow?

PRINCIPLE #4
HEALTHY BOUNDARY SYSTEMS

I have enjoyed doing a lot of research for this book and I have learned that, if you want to win heathy communication and clear expectations are extremely important.

Setting limits for screen time enable all family members to become aware of the house rules

- 2hours TV time is more than enough.
- 2hours screen time in from of additional technology is also more than enough too

When I was doing research, I learned that wealthy people usually have big libraries and small/no TV.

But poor people tend to have small/no books and a big TV. I think someone also told me that Steve Jobs children did not own iPads/iPhones etc.

Because they were too busy living life instead of trying to waste it being distracted from what is important in life. Some families leave their TV on all day, I think it is a good idea to eliminate background TV to allow you to enjoy quality time alone, with family and friends.

If you have favourite programs that you enjoy watching it'd would be a good idea to record programs to watch during agreed screen time periods.

I think a family meeting is the best way to agree on healthy boundaries.

- Did you know that some families do not have routines, are in constant chaos and frequently deal with crisis.

During my research I have come to learn that parents who have experienced a host of childhood traumas tend to either bed extremely strict and controlling or fail by enforcing little or no rules or boundaries.

Discuss ways to create new strengths that can help you and your family to develop healthy boundary systems.

I really believe that family's need healthy boundaries so that all family members know what is expected of them.

My suggestion to you and your family to create healthy boundary systems:

- Healthy communication and listening skills are a good starting point

- Take time to affirm and support each other as much as possible

- Be clear about your desired outcomes and how to achieve them

- Respect each other for your different skills and abilities

- Learn to develop a sense of trust

- It is so important to have a sense of play and humour within your family

- It is important to have a sense of shared responsibility

- Discuss what is right and wrong with your family

- Discuss how to create a healthy balance of interaction for all family members

- It is so important to respect the privacy of each family member

- It is important to value being of service to others

- Come up with some quality time spent around a family table to engage in conversations.

- Come up with some ideas for leisure time for you and your family.

- Come up with some ways that you and your family can admit to mistakes and do some research on possible solution to problems

Agree on some healthy boundaries for you and your family. These boundaries should support you and your family to create the lifestyle that you all desire to experience.

Discuss these with your family:

- How can we set achievable goals by addressing one issue at a time?
- How can we learn to be a good role model to each other?
- How can we give second chances/forgive?
- How can we hire coaches and mentors for different areas in our lives?
- How can we build each other's confidence by using solution focused approaches to identify and celebrate each of our successes?
- How can we problem solve during family meetings and establish age appropriate consequences?
- How can we listen actively, validate thoughts, feelings and ideas etc.?
- How can we openly discuss expectations of each family member?
- How can we ask open-ended questions that will encourage discussions?
- How can we frequently discuss future plans and what needs to be

put in place to achieve our desired outcomes?
- How can we discuss our strengths and weaknesses without anyone feeling uncomfortable?
- How can we talk more about what life was like when our parents were our age?

Discuss your opinions with your family and friends

PRINCIPLE #5
BASICS NEEDS

Over the years, my family and I have attended a lot of personal development events and
we have learned so much about ourselves, each other and others.

**You can see in the acknowledgement section some of the wonderful mentors we have.
You can GOOGLE them to find out more of their special skills**

I truly believe that it is very important to have an understanding of our basic human needs,
in order to feel happy and fulfilled in life.

Did you know that we all have basic human needs? Here are some of our basic human needs. Yes food, water and a home are also important. But did you know the following basic human needs?

- Certainty: Is a desire for a guaranteed outcome that will either create pain or pleasure
- Praise: Is a desire to feel acknowledged and respected
- Uncertainty: Is a desire for change.
- Contribution: Is a desire to be of service to others.
- Encouragement: Is a desire to feel supported
- Connection: Is a desire to connect with others and not feel alone.
- Love: Is a desire to give and to receive love.
- Safety: Is a desire to feel safe and protected.
- Significance: Is a desire to feel important and seen as a unique, special and worthy.
- Growth: Is a desire to obtain knowledge for example embarking on a journey of self-discovery.

I think praise, encouragement, certainty, uncertainty, contribution, connection, love, safety and growth make us feel good and when we learn to find health ways to fulfil these basic needs this is the difference that makes the difference in our lives.

Ask yourself how do you currently fulfil your needs for each of the above?

If you fulfil some of your basic needs in an unhealthy way, what can you choose to do differently?

Just for the record we all need food, water and a home to live in. The above needs are different to these, I was talking about what we learned at personal development events.

- Did you know that praising and encouragement are two of the most powerful tools that we like to experience as a child?

In life it is a good idea to praise and appreciate your friends and family for who they are and for what they do.

When you do this, you are letting them know that they are appreciated and worthwhile.

Can you remember a time when someone said any of these sentences to you?

- "Thank you so much for helping me"
- "Oh wow, you are so amazing"
- "You have worked so hard for that subject"
- "Thanks for helping me"
- "I love you so much"
- "You are so cute and loving"
- "You are so adorable"
- "I have a surprise for you"
- "This evening is games night"
- "Our class won house points"
- "Reading feeds your mind"
- "You are the WINNER!"
- "You are amazing and one of a kind"

- "Thank you for making me feel safe"
- "Thank you for loving me"

Take a moment to think about how each of these sentences make you feel?

PRINCIPLE #6
GET BACK INTO THE WILD

From playing on iPads, mobile phones, tablets and watching television, nowadays children seem to be spending more and more time inside in front of a screen.
This has a negative impact on our health and development.

It is important for us to get back into the wild and play. My parents and Nan often tell me, my brothers and sisters stories about when they were our age and use to have fun all day long playing out in the wild.

Outdoor play is great for inspiring our creativity. It allows our imaginations to literally run wild. When we play outside it helps us to develop our learning abilities.

We learn through play and having fun with our friends and family, being outside in the wild encourages us to think.

When we are outside playing in the wild, there's so much space and I always enjoy running around with my family and friends.

When I am out in the wild I have so much fun and I enjoy making new friends. It is very important for you to participate in games and activities outside in the wild because it allows you to practice your social skills.

Being outside in the wild also helps you to learn independence while socialising with other children or by ourselves.

When outside in the wild we learn to explore, pick ourselves up when we fall, and it teaches us independence and to be self-reliant.

There are so many health benefits linked to playing outside in the wild. Because outdoor play allows us to be more active. Which helps us to build strong bones and good fitness levels and if you are anything like me, I tend to burn off a lot of energy.

It's such an awesome feeling to play outside in the sunshine and in the snow too.
- Think about what you enjoy doing outside in the wild and with who?

I really enjoy the freedom of playing outside in the wild. it makes me feel so happy and relaxed.

- **Did you know that you get vitamin D from playing outside in the sunshine?**

When I go out into the wild to play it helps to improve my moods and creates a positive mental attitude. The good news for your parents is that, you will be tired after having lots of fun outside in the wild and will go to bed on time.

When I start to bounce around the house like a Bouncing, Bouncing Tigger my mum knows that it is time for me to go out into the wild.

The freedom out in the wild lets me get rid of built up energy, I usually become fidgety when I sit in one place for long periods of time.

Being outside in the wild helps me to become calm and helps to improve my focus.

My name is not Paolo Ben Salmi aka Pint Size Adventurer for no reason.

I absolutely love being outside in the wild so I can explore. I love to explore when I am on my own, with family and with old and new friends.

- Where do you like to explore and with who?

Playing outside in the wild can help you to learn to step outside your comfort zone and expand your boundaries and become good at-risk assessment.

It can also teach you to explore new games and become confident in learning to try new things without being guided by adults.

- Are you ready to come out into the wild to have fun, make new friends and explore?

PRINCIPLE #7
I READ THEREFORE I AM

I encourage you to have interests, hobbies and to read good age appropriate books.

I read therefore I am... once upon a time I use to dislike reading. I used to find it boring and I would always get upset and refuse to read when my mum and teachers asked me to read.

My mum was worried, she thought I was struggling to read so she sat me down and asked me what the problem was.
I did not find it hard to read in fact I was a good reader.
I just use to hate reading boring books, so I asked for books that I liked and now I love reading books that interest me.

When I went to school I chose to read, I went from being on a lowest reading level in my class and I passed all the reading levels and achieved a FREE READERS pass in one day.

My teacher was in total shock, and she said that I was amazing at reading. I am now allowed to read any book in my school library or bring in a book of my choice.
This made me feel really happy and now I know how important it is to read.

- Did you know that reading at least 25 pages per day will help you to enjoy reading more?

I read therefore I AM. I read therefore I am smart. I read therefore I am expanding. I read therefore I am happy. I read therefore I am learning new things.

- When was the last time you read a book?

Just like any other muscle in your body, your brain requires exercise to keep it strong and healthy this is why reading, playing chess and puzzles are so important.

- Have you ever heard the phrase "use it or lose it"?

Let's face it life can become stressful at times. The good news is that no matter how stressed you feel it all just slips away when you lose yourself in a great story.

Reading novel can take you on an adventure and before you know it you will feel calm and relaxed.

Everything you read fills your head with new information, and you will have access to that information throughout your life. The more you read the more knowledge you will have access to, in life people can to take many things from you

- The question is what is the one thing that can never be taken from you?

The answer is knowledge, because no one can take your knowledge from you.

The more you read, the more words you add to your toolbox, ready and waiting to be used by you every day in your vocabulary.
Being able to communicate with a wide range of words will help your life as a Pint Size Adventurer and will increase your confidence.

- Did you know that people who are well spoken and who are knowledgeable tend to get promotions quicker than their peers and go on to become successful in business.

- Did you know that when you read a book, you have to remember a lot of words, grammar and so much more and this all improves your memory. Our brains are amazing because there is no limit to what it can remember with ease.

- The question is what are you knowledge are you choosing to fill your brain with?

Can you remember a time when you were watching or reading something, and you were able to solve the mystery before everyone else? This is because Pint Size Adventurers who read a lot exercise their analytical thinking skills. This is done by your brain learning to take note of all the details provided and sorting them out for example

"opportunityisnowhere"

Our brains are so amazing it can work out things quickly

- What sentence can you read above?

Opportunity is no where or Opportunity is now here?

Our brain does this automatically and gets better at doing this the more we read.

Try to read this (just relax and read normally)

"Aoccdrnig to a rscheearch at Cmabrigde Uinervtisy, it deosn't mttaer in waht oredr the ltteers in a wrod are, the olny iprmoatnt tihng is taht the frist and lsat ltteers be at the rghit pclae. The rset can be a toatl mses and you can sitll raed it wouthit porbelm. Tihs is bcuseae the huamn mnid deos not raed ervey lteter by istlef, but the wrod as a wlohe."

YOU ARE AN AWESOME PINT SIZE ADVENTURER – WELL DONE FOR READING IT CORRECTLY.

This is not my words I am quoting them from this website: http://www.foxnews.com/story/2009/03/31/if-can-raed-tihs-msut-be-raelly-smrat.html

DID YOU GET IT?

Reading is a good way to relax too. It can help you to experience inner peace, fun, excitement and adventure etc.

Pint Size Adventurer reading can be so much fun. There is are so many reading books filled with so much adventure for you to enjoy.

So why don't you choose to step away from screen time, pick up a book and go on an adventure of your choice?

-   The question is what book could you write? Becoming an author can be so much fun and it will create a lot of opportunities for you too.

- Do you know how to improve your focus and concentration?

Well, I will give you a clue...

"Read a _ _ _ _"

Yes, that's right Pint Size Adventurer
"Read A Book"

When you read a book, all of your attention is focused on the words on the page.
It's like the rest of the world just slips away into the distant background and you go off into an adventure. I challenge you to participate in my 21 Day Pint Size Adventurer Challenge to read 25, details of my products and services can be found at the back of the book. You'll be surprised at how much more focused you become.

Frequent reading will improve your hand writing abilities because you will improve your writing style.

READING FEEDS YOUR MIND

PRINCIPLE #8
SOCIALISE

I believe that it is a very good idea to reduce the use of technology and socialise with friends and family because it is very important to spend quality time together.

You could also ask your parents to record your favourite programs so you can watch them when you have the agreed screen time.

Always talk to your parents about the sites that your friends tell you to visit just to get a better understating of the content on the website.

I really believe that our parents care about us very much and they just want to ensure that we feed our brains with age appropriate content.

I often ask my mum and siblings to play with me on my iPad, computer and watch my favourite TV programs with me because it is fun and like them to be a part of what I enjoy doing.

I think playdates are really important for Pint Size Adventurers of all ages.

Talk to your parents about arranging playdates with friends and family that you enjoy spending time with and also to make new friends.

Playdates make you feel as if you have something to look forward to especially if you come from aa big family like me. It's always nice to do things together and separately.

Socialising more with friends can help me to build a stronger bond with friends. Because when you have fun and experience things with someone, you feel more connected to them.

All families are different, all homes are different, and we all eat different things and do things.

Socialising is a good at your friends homes is an awesome way to experience new and exciting things.

I really enjoy going to visit my friends' homes because it is an adventure for me to experience a new environment.

I enjoy getting to know my friend's parents.

The next time you go on a playdate, notice the different foods they eat, how they communicate,

thigs they say and do, the different house rules and the size of their family etc.

PRINCIPLE #9
BED TIME RUTINE

- Did you know that it is very important to stop being in front of a screen for at least 2 hours before your bedtime.

- This will allow your brain to relax just before you sleep.

It is also a very, very, very, very, very come on say it with a very good idea to talk to your parents about agreeing on screen-free days

If you are anything like me when it comes to bed time I use to say:

- "Oh… but I don't want to go to bed. Why does Lashai and Tray-Sean get to stay up later, It's not fair. Just let me …."

- "Can I just finish playing chess?"

- "None of my friends go to bed at 8pm on a school night"

- "Can I have a drink?"

- "I need to go to the toilet"

Ha, ha, ha why oh why do we do this to ourselves and to our parents?

Why do we resist going to bed on time? If this is you I challenge you to go to bed on time to get a good night rest and to see the reaction on your parents faces. Also, this is an excellent opportunity to earn brownie points because you will allow your parents to relax which will give them more energy to play with you the next day.

Going to bed on time will help you to build a healthy relationship with your parents. Use this time to have a conversation with your family just before bed for a few minutes of undivided attention

I am now 8yrs old and I like to think that I am independent and have the skills to settle myself down when it is bed time.

I now understand that Bedtime routines help me to transition from the busy activities of the day and just drift off to sleep. I also look forward to bedtime as a way to be connected with my mum or older sister when we talk just before bed or my older brother (because we share a room together).

Try to read before you sleep, I enjoy talking just before falling asleep, It helps me stay connected in a positive way just before I drift off to sleep.

Like everything else about family life, the goal isn't to be perfect around bedtime routines.

Communication is always a good idea, talk to your family about what helps you to drift off to sleep.

Let's face it, bedtime is often anything but a relaxed calm ending to the day we'd like it to be.

Our 4yr old brother doesn't like going to bed on and I am sure you can imagine what a 4yr old does to escape ha, ha, ha, ha….

- Do you know the recommended sleeps periods for your age?

I learned that this is what is recommended

- Ages 3-5yrs are recommended 10-13hrs sleep

- Ages 6-13yrs are recommended 9-11 hrs sleep

- Ages 14-17yrs are recommended 8-10hrs sleep

- Ages 18-25yrs are recommended 7-9hrs sleep

It is very important to get enough sleep at night because it will affect your **Learning, health, mood and memory** etc.

Sleep helps our brains to organise new information to memory through a process called memory consolidation. **Sleep** deprivation can make you to put on weight because a lack of sleep will affect the way your body processes and stores nutriments from foods such as carbohydrates etc.

If you do not get enough sleep at night you will fall asleep during the day and this could happen anywhere.

A lack of Sleep can make you irritable, impatient, affect your concentration and become moody.

Too little sleep can also leave you too tired to do the things you like to do.

So, do you now understand the importance of a bedtime routine?

After all your parents just want the best for you.

PRINCIPLE #10
BE IN THE CHOICE

- How can you learn to be in the choice?
- Choose how you want to spend your day?
- Do you have a hobby, if not choose one?
- What do you enjoy doing in your spare time and with who?
-

Speak to your family about what you can do as a family to create a healthy balance of computer and television use.

You could look at it this way screen time vs active time and at what cost?

Discuss some of the health and social difficulties that using technology may cause for you, your family and friends.

Ask your parents to talk to you about how much TV they were allowed to watch on a school night.
Ask what rules they had to honour when they you're your age and what benefits they can now see but did not realise at the time

- Shhh... can you keep a secret Pint Size Adventurer?

This is one of my favourite conversations.

I just love talking to my mum about how I earn additional screen time from time to time by helping out at home etc.

Talk to your parents about creating a daily timetable for homework, screen time and outdoor play etc.

Ask your parents if you can spend at least 10 minutes every day with each playing, talking or doing something that you choose to do.
The golden rule is it cannot involve a screen, it is very important to cuddle and just look into each other's eyes without being distracted by a screen which takes the focus of each other.

Say it with Meeee

"IT'S NOW TIME TO GET OFF YOUR iPad And Back Into The WILD!.."

Paolo Ben Salmi
aka Pint Size Adventurer

Do you ever find yourself say

"Oooohh I'm bored!......"

If the answer is YES!

Then I have some ideas on how to go about entertaining yourself

I believe that it is a good idea to choose activities that best fit your personality.

ACTIVITY IDEAS

Indoor Activities for Homebound Pint Size Adventurers

- Build an indoor obstacle course
- Play chess
- Exercise
- Read
- Create your own puzzle
- Find an age appropriate tutorial on YouTube (ask for your parents' for their permission)
- Ask an adult to help you to rearrange your bedroom
- Play some music and dance like no one is watching
- Play Simon Says
- Create a performance to share with your family

Innovative Actives For Innovative Pint Size Adventurers

- Act out your favourite book
- Write your own book
- Come up with a business idea
- Do some baking (ask an adult to help with the oven and any dangerous equipment)
- Bring out the pots and pans and practice drumming skills.
- Build new structures and objects out of LEGOs (without using the instructions).
- Compose a poem
- Create a community project to help others in need
- Design -- and fill in -- your own mad libs.
- Publish a pretend newspaper.
- Write a gratitude letter to someone special to express how much you appreciate them (e.g. your parents, siblings, grandparents etc

Food Focused Activates For Master Chef Pint Size Adventurers

- Bake cookies
- Cook an entire meal ask your parents to help
- Bake bread
- Make homemade ice cream
- Bake Fairy cakes
- Bake muffins
- Make vegetable and fruit smoothies Yummy….yum…yum…

Active Activities For Active Pint Size Adventurers

- Spend the day at your local swimming pool
- Go to a mini golf course
- Go karting
- Play football
- Play basketball
- Play tennis
- Ride a bike
- Play catch
- Roller skate
- Roller blade.
- Run relay races
- Spend the day in the park
- Throw around the Frisbee with some friends

Thought Provoking Activities For Child Genius
Pint Size Adventurers

- Write an A4 page detailing the lifestyle you desire to create when you grow up
- Research experts in an industry that interests you
- Explore the world with Google Maps (ask for your parents' permission first)
- Do some research at your local library (ask your parent to take you)
- Teach yourselves Sign Language (ASL) alphabet.
- Visit an interactive museum.

This is a photo of the 20 Finalist of Channel 4 Child Genius 2017.

My older brother, Tray-Sean is on the back row top right-hand corner, with Richard Osman was one of them !

I am so proud of him, my big **BRO** !

Creative Activities For Creative Pint Size Adventurers

- Blow homemade bubble (find the step by step online)
- Make a sun dial
- Create bubble paint prints
- Draw cool murals
- **Give your parents a make over**
- Create a flower arrangement for the dining room table.
- Take creative photos indoors and outdoors
- Tie-dye a T-shirt !

Exploration Activities For Adventurous Pint Size Adventurers

- Visit your local farmers' market and discover interesting products you've never seen before.
- Put together some items to put into a time capsule and bury it in your garden
- Set up a lemonade stand.
- Visit www.365tickets.com for an adventurous day out with your family
- Visit www.kidzania.co.uk to plan a fun day out with your family
- Ask your parents to visit www.merlinannualpass.co.uk to purchase an annual pass for your family (come up with some ideas to raise the money to pay for the tickets)
-

Outdoor Activities For Wild Pint Size Adventurers

- Discovery insects and wildlife in your garden
- Country walk
- Camp out in your garden
- Visit a farm
- Visit a zoo
- Have a picnic with family and friends
- Plant a tree
- Research different types of birds in your area
- Start a mini garden
- Explore nature.
- Walk on the beach and collect seashells.

I hope these ideas inspire you

CREATE YOUR OWN SCREEN TIME RULES

Did you know that rules help to create healthy boundaries within your family.

To create your own screen time rules simply choose one screen time bad habit that you have and replace it with a good screen time habit.

Then come up with some rules that will help you to reduce your screen time and get outside into the wild to have fun, explore and make new friends.

For example "Every day complete homework before watching TV"

List 10 new rules below:

1) _____

2) _____

3) _____

4) _____

5) _____

6) _____

7) _____

8) _____

9) _____

10) _____

ABOUT THE AUTHOR

PAOLO BEN SALMI

"There's two types of adventures : 1 Going out into the wild and exploring and 2 Going on an inwards journey self-discovery"
Paolo Ben Salmi

10 year-old Child Advocate Paolo Ben Salmi aka Pint Size Adventurer is an award-winning author of Pint Size Adventurer - 10 Keys Principles To Get Your KIDS off their iPads & Into The Wild, 2nd place in TruLittle Heros Award - U12 Entrepreneur 2017, Former International Radio Show host, 229/17. Paolo is *the youngest ever Water-to-Go™™ Ambassador and founder of The Abundant Adventure Creator™*

Paolo made history by being the youngest person to interview Dr John Demartini:

https://www.facebook.com/350400542063654/videos/363072487463126/

Google Dr John De Martini and you can find out more about this great Mentor.

I am here as your Personal developments coach and founder of Pint Size Adventurer who is here to help you to plant the seed toward self-discovery, exploration of the internal and external world and adventurer in abundance via a variety of products and services to assist you to create a brighter future

Paolo aims to inspire you fill your life with an abundance of adventures both outside in the wild and inward into your own personal journey of self-discovery.

Paolo dreams of becoming an engineer, he enjoys Quantum Physics, Theatre, Bike Riding, Go Karting, Sports Cars, Participating in Sports, Playing Chess, visiting places such as Eton College, Legoland and Chessington World of Adventures etc

Paolo is the second youngest of five siblings: LASHAI, TRAY-SEAN, YASMINE and AMIRE

Together they are known as

"The Fantastic Five"

WELL DONE FOR READING PINT SIZE
ADVENTURER – 10 KEY PRINCIPLES TO
GET YOUR KIDS OFF THEIR iPAD AND
INTO THE WILD.

PLEASE LEAVE A REVIEW FOR THE
BOOK ON AMAZON

I KNOW
YOU ARE AWESOME !

I hope one day I can meet you.

NOW MY FAMILY
ARE GOING
TO SHARE
SOME BONUS
INFORMATION
WITH
YOU

Surprise Bonus: DID YOU KNOW?

Did YOU know that we all develop our belief systems about ourselves and the world around us from our environment?

Our family and friends, role models, television, magazines and advertising can either be nurturing or damaging.

It is important that we, our families and our friends learn to take control of our belief systems and the younger that we do, the easier it is.

It can be as simple as affirming the positive beliefs that we would like to grow up with. Negative beliefs can impact our lives greatly and can be hard to shift as we grow older.

Affirmations are a powerful and holistic way of building positive mind and happier children and will go onto help them through their lives.

This will also nurture their authentic self and help them to enjoy the magic of childhood.

Put simply, Because I Am Intelligent - 365 Affirmations To Brighten Up Your Day aims to affirm to one's self positive words that are absorbed by the mind to create your belief system.

Once affirmations are learned, they work by coming to mind when that belief is challenged.

For example if your affirmation is
"I am wonderful just the way I am",
and you are told you are stupid,
the affirmation will come to mind to remind you of
your belief.

Instead, you will think,
"I'm not stupid, I am wonderful!"

Without a positive belief, you may take on the one
you just heard and start to believe that you are
stupid.
The more an affirmation is repeated, positive or
negative, the stronger it becomes.

ABOUT THE BEN SALMI FAMILY

Sabrina Ben Salmi BSc
BYA Mother of The Year Award Winner

Is a proud mother of
5 Entrepreneurial children aged 6 to 19 years old who she
referees to as her
Fantastic 5.

Sabrina is a Multi-Award Winning Author, Business &
Personal Development Consultant, Founding directors of an
Ofsted rated Outstanding school: Harris Invictus Academy
(Secondary).
Former Radio Show Host, Public Speaker. Founder of The
Conscious Entrepreneur Blueprint™, Dreaming Big
Together – Mamas Secret Recipe™ & Shift Happens™.

Sabrina Ben Salmi BSc is here to empower you to plant the
seed so that you and your family can learn to Dream Big
Together via a variety of products and services that aim to
assist you and your loved ones to create a brighter future.
Sabrina and her children have been featured in the media
Internationally via Radio, TV, Newspapers, magazines etc to
name a few Channel 4 documentaries:
Secret Millionaire/Child Genius, BBC London News, LBC
Radio, BBC Radio, Fabulous Magazine etc.

"It's about time that we stop granting our children indefinite
leave to remain on the streets and empower them to plant the
seed for a brighter tomorrow"

Mohamed Ben Salmi
Is a proud father of
3 and 2 step Entrepreneurial children aged 6 to 19 years
old

Speaks Arabic/French/English, author of 'A Mirror of Happiness' and has a passion for music, travel, languages, meeting new people and biology.

Lashai Ben Salmi
aka Dreampreneur
is a 19 years old

AS SEEN OF TV, RADIO & NEWSPAPERS (BBC Korea:

https://www.facebook.com/818434098337843/posts/12210 18028079446?sfns=mo) etc. Lashai Ben Salmi aka DREAMPRENEUR is not your average 18yr old.

She is a multi-award winning Youth Advocate, Property Mentor & Investor, Presented award for TruLittle Heros Award 2018, Social Media Content Creator for The Korean Cultural Centre, Winner of TruLittle Heros Award - Entrepreneur 2017 and Speaker at Virgin Money Lounge Historical Black History Month first ever event.

Lashai is founder of Stepping Stones Publishing House.

Lashai hosts her signature program called Stepping Stones at Virgin Money Lounge

The Beat You Expo (15,000 attendees), Mentioned in Carolyn A Brent book called: Across All Ages DEEP BEAUTY Lashai is one of 14 VIP names mentioned which is in the congress library in Washington DC.

Guest Speaker at Mercedes Benz World 10th April 2018, High Profile Club, YouTuber with 26K plus subscribers and over 4M plus views (Korean Channel), An award winning author of Kidz That Dream Big, Andy Harrington ACE Coach, Former International Radio Show host, Winner of

Regan Hillyer International Scholarship, a speaker. Lashai is a Regan Hillyer International Team Member, a business/personal developments Consultant.

Founder of Blossom Tree Photography & Videography Produced content in association with Legoland Resort, Harry Potter, Little Mix and Disney Pixar, Sony, Warner Brothers & Universal etc.

Co-founder of A Precipice of A Dream and founder of Put The RED Card Up To bullying & My Journey - Giving Youth Several Reasons to Smile who is here to help children and youth to plant the seed for an abundance of unique opportunities via a variety of products and services to assist you to create a brighter future

If you are looking for an inspiring, wise, talented, refreshing and powerful speaker then 18yr old Lashai Ben Salmi is guaranteed to make a big impact at your event. Lashai has been a part of the personal development world since the age of 11yrs.

Lashai has a burning desire to transform lives with her stage presence, knowledge and wisdom! Lashai's signature topics include: Congruency, Alignment, Self-Belief, YouTube, Social Media, Connection, Inspiration and Motivation.

Lashai's signature program: The Stepping Stone's Formula™ & YouSmart - How To Work Smart, Not Hard On YouTube™

Lashai's Books:

1. Kidz That Dream Big: Dreams Do Come True
https://www.amazon.co.uk/dp/1912547066/ref=cm_sw_r_
cp_api_mwbUAbS8BTQHE

2. Kidz That Dream Big!...
https://www.amazon.co.uk/dp/1909039322/ref=cm_sw_r_cp_api_i_eMZKCbNSJ3JDX

3. KIDZ THAT DREAM BIG!: The Stepping Stones Formula™
https://www.amazon.co.uk/dp/B07NJ8YLHM/ref=cm_sw_r_cp_api_i_RMZKCbG7CXZBJ

Facebook page: Kidz That Dream Big:
https://www.facebook.com/Kidz-that-Dream-BIG-154694734627138/

**Tray-Sean Ben Salmi
aka I'm That KID
is a 14 years old**

AS SEEN ON TV, RADIO, MAGAZINES & NEWSPAPERS etc.

Tray-Sean Ben Salmi aka I'm That KID is not your average 14yr old. Tray-Sean Ben Salmi is a 14yr old Amazon #1 Best Seller & Award Winning Author, Stock & Shares Trader, Property Mentor & Investor, Award winning Public Speaker (Virgin, The Beat You Expo 15,000 attendees) and Child Advocate. Tray-Sean has recently signed a contract with FirstPoint USA 🇺🇸 for an opportunity to go to America for a full academic and sports scholarship

Child Genius 2017 top 20 smartest children in the UK as a result Tray-Sean was 1 out of 34 boys to be invited to sit papers at the prestigious Eton College.

Tray-Sean is founder of Influencer Publishing House.

Tray-Sean hosts his signature program called I'm That KID at Virgin Money Lounge

Tray-Sean is an award winning author of Kidz That Dream Big, Former Radio Show host, Regan Hillyer International Be Your Brand Fellow, Author of 10 Seconds To Child Genius, Winner of TruLittle Heros Award - Academic, Business/Personal developments mentor & coach.

Tray-Sean participated in brand campaigns for Sainsburys, Legoland, Warner Bros, Sony and Official Judges for Made For Mums Toy Awards to name a few.

Tray-Sean is founder of I'm That KID covers:

- I'm That KID - Bridging The Gap Between Fathers & Sons™
- I'm That KID – Creating A Vision Board for My Future™
- I'm That KID – Taking The Stage™
- I'm That KID - Inspiring My Community To Pay It Forward™
- I'm That KID - There's A Book Inside ME™
- I'm That KID - Families That Play Together Stay Together™
- I'm That KID - Empowering You To Step Into Your POWER™
- I'm That KID - BEING The Change That I Desires To See In The World™

10 Seconds To Child Genius is a book series co-founded by Tray-Sean Ben Salmi & Philip Chan. This book series aims to help children and young people to plant the seed today to create a brighter future tomorrow.

Q : How do you know what you DON'T KNOW?
A : When someone point out the obvious which you have overlooked!

PAOLO BEN SALMI aka PINT SIZE ADVENTURER

There is a mis-conception that only a limited amount of people can be a 'Child Genius'. In this book Tray-Sean Ben Salmi show you this 'myth' is not true.

JUST KNOW THAT YOU CAN HELP YOUR CHILD TO DISCOVER THEIR GENIUS WITHIN.

Tray-Sean's signature program: I'M That KID Blueprint™

Tray-Sean's Books:

1. 10 Seconds To Child Genius
https://www.amazon.co.uk/dp/099286948X/ref=cm_sw_r_cp_api_uxbUAbPH5C3K1

2. I'm That KID: Empowering You to Step Into Your Power
https://www.amazon.co.uk/dp/B07PXFS7TY/ref=cm_sw_r_cp_api_i_TGZKCb0188EG1

3. 10 Seconds To Child Genius: The Road To Child Genius
https://www.amazon.co.uk/dp/B07PXBS2MQ/ref=cm_sw_r_cp_api_i_CIZKCbDFPKRF7

4. 10 Seconds To Child Genius: From Eton Road To Eton College
https://www.amazon.co.uk/dp/B07P9K469N/ref=cm_sw_r_cp_api_i_rJZKCb951S2FV

5. Kidz That Dream Big!...
https://www.amazon.co.uk/dp/1909039322/ref=cm_sw_r_cp_api_i_-JZKCbYJFFCAD

6. Kidz That Dream Big: Dreams Do Come True
https://www.amazon.co.uk/dp/1912547066/ref=cm_sw_r_cp_api_i_9KZKCbD0XTRYA

7. Property Problem Solver: Has Your Property Become A Pain In Your Life?
https://www.amazon.co.uk/dp/B07Q7WX3MY/ref=cm_s
w r cp api i 1cGOCb2XT7BEP

Facebook page: 10 Seconds To Child Genius:
https://m.facebook.com/10secondstochildgenius/
We are so proud of him

Yasmine Ben Salmi
aka LovePreneur
is an 12 years old

AS SEEN OF TV, RADIO & NEWSPAPERS etc
Yasmine Ben Salmi aka LovePreneur is an 11yr award winning author of The Choice is Your - 10 Keys Principles To Create A Happier Lifestyle and Winner of TruLittle Heros Award - Creative 2017.

Guest Speaker at Best You Expo (15,000 attendees) and Former International Radio Show Host.

Yasmine is the founder of The Choice Is Yours Publishing House.

Yasmine hosts her signature program called The Choice Is Yours - Your Thinking C.A.P For Living & Loving Life at Virgin Money Lounge

Yasmine participated in campaigns for Sainsburys, Legoland, Warner Bros, Sony and Made For Mums to name a few.

Yasmine's signature program: Your Thinking C.A.P For Living & Loving Life™

Yasmine is founder of Dog Walking Service "Woof-Woof your dog is here".

Yasmine was nominated for a R.E.E.B.A Award 2017, Winner of Radio Works Authors Awards 2017 and nominated for National Diversity Award 2017.

Yasmine is also the founder of Mother and Daughter Connect Collection and founder of Lovepreneure.

Yasmine dreams to be the change that she desires to see in the world and inspire others to be in the choice as often as possible.

The question is when will you start living life on your terms?

Yasmine's Books:

- The Choice Is Yours: 10 Key Principles to Create a Happier Lifestyle
https://www.amazon.co.uk/dp/1912547082/ref=cm_sw_r_cp_api_JbaUAbR7K3MNS

- The Choice Is Yours: Your Thinking C.A.P For Living & Loving
https://www.amazon.co.uk/dp/1912999048/ref=cm_sw_r_cp_api_i_5NZKCb3D9TGNY

Facebook page: Lovepreneure:
https://m.facebook.com/YasmineBenSalmiakaLovePrenur/

Paolo Ben Salmi
aka Pint Size Adventurer
is 10 years old

AS SEEN OF TV, RADIO & NEWSPAPERS

10yr old Paolo Ben Salmi aka Pint Size Adventurer is a Water-to-Go's youngest ever ambassador! https://www.watertogo.eu/paolobensalmi

blog about Water-to-Go and Paolo: https://www.watertogo.eu/blog/meet-paolo-water-to-gos-youngest-ever-ambassador/

Paolo is the founder of Adventurous Publishing House.

Paolo hosts her signature program called Pint Size Adventurer - The Abundant Adventure Creator at Virgin Money Lounge

Paolo Ben Salmi is an award winning author of Pint Size Adventurer - 10 Keys Principles To Get Your KIDS off their iPads & Into The Wild.

Paolo is an Award Winning Public Speaker (who has spoken at eleventh such as Mercedes Benz World and Virgin etc).

Paolo has participated in brand campaigns for Sainsburys, Legoland, Warner Bros, Sony and Made For Mums to name a few.

Paolo's signature program is called The Abundant Adventure Inventor™

TruLittle Heros Award - U12 Entreprenur 2017, Guest Speaker at The Beat You Expo (15,000 attendees)

Mercedes Benz World 10th April, Official Judge for Made For Mums Toy Awards 2018 via Team Trouble, Former International Radio Show host

2017 Paolo made history by being the youngest to interview Dr John Demartini: https://www.facebook.com/350400542063654/videos/3630 72487463126/

Personal developments coach and founder of Pint Size Adventurer who is here to help you to plant the seed toward self-discovery, exploration of the internal and external world and adventurer in abundance via a variety of products and services to assist you to create a brighter future. Paolo desires to encourage as many children as possible to go on adventures both internally and externally to activate their natural curiosity.

The question is are you watching the movie, in the movie or directing the movie?

Paolo's Books:

1. Pint Size Adventurer: 10 Key Principles To Get Your KIDS off Their iPads & Into The Wild
https://www.amazon.co.uk/dp/1912547031/ref=cm_sw_r_ cp_api_iwXXAbMZRM7QA

2. Pint Sized Adventurer: The Abundant Adventure Creator
https://www.amazon.co.uk/dp/1912999056/ref=cm_sw_r_ cp_api_i_YOZKCbXBNE59T

Facebook page: Pint Size Adventurer:
https://m.facebook.com/paolobensalmiakapintsizeadventure r/

Amire Ben Salmi
aka Mr Because I AM Intelligent
is a 6 years old

AS SEEN OF TV, RADIO & NEWSPAPERS etc

Amire Ben Salmi aka Mr Because I AM Intelligent is a 6yr old award winning author of Because I AM Intelligent - 365 Affirmations To Brighten Up Your Day. Amire was a guest Speaker at The Beat You Expo (15,000 attendees).

Amire is the founder of I AM Publishing House

Amire hosts his signature program called Because I AM Intelligent - Easy As P.I.E Affirmations at Virgin Money Lounge. Amire has participated in campaigns for Sainsburys, Legoland, Warner Bros and Sony to name a few.

Amires signature program is Easy-As-P.I.E Affirmations™

Amire is founder of Because I AM Intelligent who is here to help you to plant the seed toward having fun learning during childhood, Positive Affirmations, Fun and Creativity in abundance via a variety of products such as a book with a matching colour car and 52 affirmation cards to assist you to create a brighter future.

Amire enjoys having fun learning with affirmations and he believes that words are very powerful.

The question is when will you choose to affirm your life?

Amire's Books:

• Because I AM Intelligent 365 Affirmations To Brighten Up Your Day

https://www.amazon.co.uk/dp/1912547023/ref=cm_sw_r_
cp_api_gcaUAb6A5W5SJ
- Because I AM Intelligent: Easy As P.I.E Affirmations
https://www.amazon.co.uk/dp/1912999005/ref=cm_sw_r_
cp_api_i_uPZKCb14F8W6W

Facebook page: Because I AM Intelligent:
https://m.facebook.com/BecauseIAMIntelligent/

Mary Paul
grandmother
AS SEEN OF TV, RADIO & NEWSPAPERS etc

Author and Award winning speaker Mary Paul is former radio show host.

Mary is an award winning public speaker, author and the founder of MARY PAUL.

Mary produces bespoke art and furniture for the high end market.

Mary became a single parent and her child needed a lot of care due to childhood illnesses. Mary launched a community project with to get the community engaged and her furniture was perturbed in the newspaper with the Queen of Jordan. Mary has exhibited her furniture in exhibitions such as Hidden Aart, 100% Design and Top Draw to name a few.

Mary has many dreams and desires to live the legacy and then leave a legacy for generations to come.

The inspiration behind MARY PAUL was to end, once and for all, what she saw as " the dubious concept of so called single parenthood".

Mary desired to make her mark and felt that expressing herself through the medium of art. Be that furniture, paintings, home staging, personal stylist that was the difference that made the difference for her and her clients. Mary is a family woman and is now a proud mother of one daughter and 5 grandchildren. Mary believes that self-care is the core essence of success.

She desires to touch the hearts of others and inspire them to enhance their personal style, their home and their garden.

The question is when will you choose to pour into your own life, so much so that you can share with others as your cup runneth over?

Mary's Book:
The Carers Blueprint: 10 Key Principles To Improve The Quality of Life For The Person You Care For
https://www.amazon.co.uk/dp/1912999099/ref=cm_sw_r_cp_api_i_sfsPCb6CK90PC

Facebook Page:

https://www.facebook.com/281125102563358/posts/29669
5597672975?sfns=mo

YOU CAN CONNECT WITH ALL OF US VIA SOCIAL MEDIA

OUR FAMILY BELIEFS & OUR FAMILY ANTHEM

"BEN SALMI TEAMWORK, MAKES THE DREAMWORK

We believe that there is no such thing as failure only feedback.

We also believe that the journey of one thousand miles begins with a single step in the right direction

FAMILY ANTHEM

If you want to be somebody,
If you want to go somewhere,
You better wake up and

PAY ATTENTION

I'm ready to be somebody,
I'm ready to go somewhere,
I'm ready to wake up and

PAY ATTENTION!

The question is ARE YOU?

SURPRISE BONUS ENTRY FROM 9YR OLD JAYDEN McKEAGUE @jaydens_jewels

What's your name? Jayden McKeague
How old are you? 9 years old
What does Adventure mean to you. Adventure means to me exploring and finding fun things to do in nature.
What do you do for Adventure.
I like going up mountains and exploring the big reservoir's and the valleys near my house in south wales.
How do you know you're experiencing Adventure. because I have found new places to play and explore.
What Adventures have you been on. I have been on mountain adventures and water adventures and learning to skip stone at the reservoirs.
Do you like to go on adventures alone or with friends and family. I like to go on adventure with my mum and dad so I can share the fun with them and we can skip stones on the water and find new places to explore.
What adventures do you enjoy. I like adventures where i find new places to explore and these can be on foot or via buses. I have just moved to south wales so have lots of new places to explore.
What do you think adventure mean to adults. I think it means finding out new information

and exploring new places and meeting new people.

What do you need to start doing to be adventurous. Using your imagination, playing with my toys, getting out in to nature and exploring. Getting off of gadgets and seeing the world via all my senses.

What do you need to do less of to be adventurous. Watching tv or using gadgets.

What do you need to do more of to be adventurous. Don't be afraid to explore and try new things. Use all your senses to explore.

What is your message to children and youth about adventure?

Adventure is fun and can help you to learn new things and ways of overcoming your Challenges. So don't be afraid to put down gadgets and try new things.

What is your message to adults about adventure?

Be more like a child and allow yourself to use your imagination and go explore.

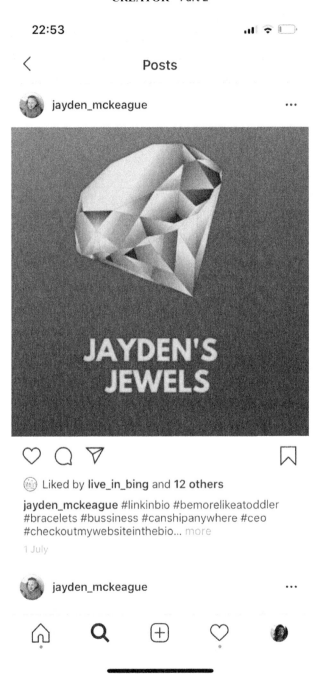

22:53

Posts

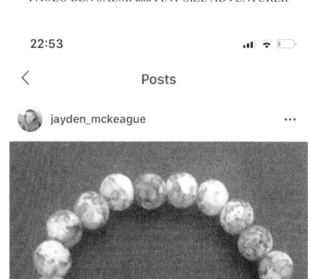

jayden_mckeague

11 likes

jayden_mckeague New stock coming soon
#yougotthis #bethechangeyouwanttosee #change
#dreambelieveachieve #empowerment... more

22:54

Posts

jayden_mckeague

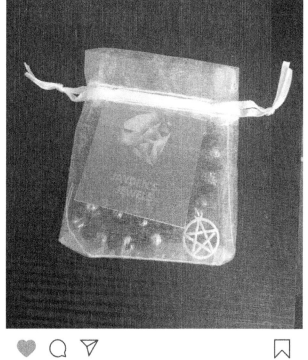

 Liked by **lovedup84** and **10 others**

jayden_mckeague First order ready to go #firstorder #bussiness #kidpreneurs #lilvee #firstofmany #bracelets

PRODUCTS & SERVICES

DO YOU WANT TO TAKE PART in THE PINT SIZE ADVENTURER 21 DAYS CHALLENGE?
– TO Get Your KIDS off their iPads & Into The Wild?

21 Days – 21 Children - £21 Gift – All For A Small Investment (ask for more details)

- You will become more focused
- You will be gifted £21 at the end of the challenge if you complete the daily challenges

THE ABUNDANT ADVENTURE CREATOR™ workshop

ADVENTUROUS PUBLISHING HOUSE
Where I publish books for Adventurers who desire to share their adventures with the world

PINT SIZE ADVENTURER VIP breakfast, lunch and dinners

PINT SIZE ADVENTURER Coaching/Mentoring for a small investment (ask for more details) to inspire YOU to have fun learning

For more information contact us:

- Facebook page: Pint Size Adventurer
- Facebook: Paolo Ben Salmi

- Instagram: Paolo Ben Salmi
- Twitter: Paolo Ben Salmi
- YouTube: Paolo Ben Salmi
- Email: paolobensalmi@gmail.com or info@adventurouspublishing.com

MY FINAL MESSAGE TO YOU:

I hope you can see
we have fun together
as a
FAMILY
and
I want my BEST FRIENDS to be
my MUM, DAD
and
MY SIBLINGS.

If we can achieve this,
SO CAN YOU !

I BELIEVE IN YOU AND WANT TO WISH YOU
ALL THE SUCCESS IN YOUR LIFE.

"STOP FOLLOWING A COMPASS YOUR
WHOLE LIFE, BECAUSE THE REAL
CUMPASS IS INSIDE OF YOU AND IT IS
YOUR HEART"

With love and Best wishes

Paolo Ben Salmi
aka Pint Size Adventurer

Printed in Great Britain
by Amazon

59440612R00088